Words or Less

Words or Less

A Short Short
History of Australia

Mr V. Slack

as dictated to Malcolm Knox

RANDOM HOUSE AUSTRALIA

Random House Australia Pty Ltd
20 Alfred Street, Milsons Point, NSW 2061
http://www.randomhouse.com.au

Sydney   New York   Toronto
London   Auckland   Johannesburg

First published by Random House Australia 2005

National Library of Australia
Cataloguing-in-Publication Entry

Knox, Malcolm, 1966–.
1788 words or less: a short short history of Australia.

ISBN 1 74051 244 8.

1. Australia – History. I. Title. II. Title: One thousand
seven hundred and eighty eight words or less.

994

Cover and internal illustrations by David Messer
Cover and internal design by Nanette Backhouse,
    saso content & design
Typeset by Midland Typesetters, Maryborough, Victoria
Printed and bound by Griffin Press, Netley, South Australia

10 9 8 7 6 5 4 3 2 1

To my teaching aides Malcolm Knox
and David Messer, who treated this book
as if it were their own

Mr Slack

What the critics said about *1788 Words or Less*

'Unrivalled in its brevity' – *Quadrant*

'History for the time-poor, cash-poor'
– *Money* magazine

'. . . makes a mockery of . . .' – Manning Clark,
author of *A Short History of Australia*

'. . . without doubt . . . the most . . . informa-
tive . . . [history] of . . . Australia . . .' – Russel
Ward, author of *The Australian Legend*

'. . . out-shorts the very shortest histories . . .'
– Don Burke

'. . . norks . . .' – *Ralph* magazine

'Sets new standards for condensation . . .'
– *Reader's Digest*

'From the moment I picked it up to the
moment I put it down I laughed, cried,
laughed again, cried again, checked the oven,
made some calls, had my hair done, laughed,
had some ladies over for lunch, and cried
again. I do so look forward to reading it . . .'
– Janette Howard

'. . . another great recipe for when friends drop
over unexpectedly . . .' – *Good Housekeeping*

Foreword

By The Rt Hon Sir John Gorton
MPKC BA LLB MGB FACE QED

If you are reading this, it means I am dead.

You see, when I was still with you I received a great number of approaches from all kinds of people for all kinds of favours, and when the chappies behind this book asked me to write a 'foreword/endorsement' I misheard their request. I thought they were a delegation from the Assemblies of God and wanted a 'four-word endorsement'. I met their word count all right: OVER MY DEAD BODY.

It eventually became clear that they were putting together some kind of history book. What, another? Australia must be the only bloody place that has more history books than history! Why can't we wait until we have a bit of a past before we start writing about it?

And besides, I wouldn't have time to read the bloody thing.

It transpired that none of this posed any kind of obstacle, as the chappies hadn't started it yet. Australian history, they told me, was a blank slate — as were their efforts to get it down on paper. What they wanted from me was my signature on a page with an official letterhead. This would serve as inspiration to get them going.

Well, I declared myself happy to oblige. Given that I was sure to be finished before they were, I thought — 'What the hell does it matter?'

So, I am afraid I cannot say much about this book. As I write, I am struggling to string two breaths together and these blighters haven't got to Captain Cook. A little disappointing for me, as the only reason I would keep reading is to see the record set straight on Bug-Eyes McMahon and that dog Fraser.

I still don't know who the hell the chappies are, but on behalf of all of us who are short of time, I commend this surprising volume to my fellow Australians. I have no doubt that this work, once finished, will meet all expectations.

1 April 2002

Contents

Prefatory Introduction: How to Use this Book #1

Welcome to Australian history! Congratulations on a wise purchase – for the price of half a kilo of flathead fillets or five crossings of the Sydney Harbour Tunnel, you have gained the priceless asset of quick, cheap knowledge. And remember, the $1.50 GST you have paid will go to our sorely underfunded hospitals and schools.

Australians need be embarrassed about our history no longer. You no longer need to hide the fact that you weren't paying attention at school and can't remember what Cook and Phillip did, which was Macquarie and which was Macarthur, why Ned Kelly didn't wear a helmet until the last day, and what the hell happened before last weekend.

In 35 years of teaching this subject, 29 as a very well-known head teacher, I have found that nothing works better than making history 'cool'. With this book I have applied my 'trade secrets' once and for all! This book is a shortcut to conveying the appearance of a well-informed, smug, complacent understanding of our great nation and its past. It contains focus group findings, primary school sources, line drawings, eye-catching design features, easy renovation tips, reading group notes and quick quizzes. Throughout, you will be asked a series of questions testing your memory – the type of questions some condescending Pom is likely to pass down the length of an aristocratic nose, starting with, 'Australian history? Pah! Isn't that an oxymoron?'

Be an oxymoron no more. Read this book or, better still, buy it, mislay it, and buy another.

Mr Slack

Introductory Preface:
How to Use this Book #2

THIS BOOK IS printed in the Bimbo typeface, first used in 1495 by the Venetian printer Andrea Di Loto for tickets employed in illegal games of chance. It was first designed for Monotype in 1929 when Benito Mussolini used it for pamphlets excoriating homosexuals, gypsies and other undesirables who stopped the trains running on time. It is printed on recycled paper from the mouldy cardboard boxes, juice containers, yellowed newspapers, magazines and used tissues you put out every Tuesday night. The size is 'small A format', which fits within all shelf widths and can be arranged in handy stacks close to the cash register at your local bookstore, to catch your eye if you've just remembered you need a birthday present for Uncle Ron and don't want to lose your place in the queue.

None of this is relevant to anything, but please, if you don't like it, don't sell it to a second-hand or remainder bookstore; seeing it on sale for less than one dollar is upsetting and humiliating to the author and illustrator and damaging to their reputation with their publisher. Use it to chock up a chair leg. Leave it at a holiday house. Store it safely in a bookshelf alongside other serious-looking history books (no-one will know from the spine). Re-gift it to a relative. Donate it to a child care centre as drawing paper. Tear up the pages to stuff inside wine glasses next time you move house. But please: you won't get anything for it in the second-hand market, so if you have to put it down, put it down humanely.

Mr Slack

Part 1

the FIRST PART

During the First Part, much happened: Australia was uncovered, settled down, explored, and upon her brown expanses were established the basic conveniences.

Those who did not die in the doing so were entitled to be proud of doing it. Convicts came and were emaciated; the resident Gonads were scattered to the five winds; Rum'n'Raisins became currency; there were civil wars and wars of incontinence; sandstone became the new granite; and brave men with their camels went to the Inland and got lost.

But before getting to the First Part, we must never forget the Other Part, which is under furious debate.

The one thing that the furious debaters agree on is that the Other Part went for a bloody long time until it came to an even bloodier end.

In fact, if Australian history was a clock, the First Part would not even start until one minute to midnight — which would make it a queer kind of clock, a pretty damn useless one to tell the truth [or to tell the time] — but anyway, this is how we do things here and if you want the whole clock and box and dice you shouldn't have come looking for the short short version you lazy bastards . . .

1. The First (But Not Original) Australians

IN THE BEGINNING a rift broke out in a valley in Africa between the Originals and the Unoriginals, who called themselves the Aboriginals as a symbol of protest and walked Out of Africa, across several Ice Ages, took a right at the Silk Road, then the second left at the Spice Road, and drove their caravans straight ahead into Colourful Exotic South-East Asia.

Being Gonadic people, the Aboriginals could not sit still. They carved canoes out of bark and rowed their gondolas to Gondolawanaland in the south, overcharging and working on their song lines until they rhymed.

They were the first Boat People. Gondolawanaland had a No Boat People policy, or Terra Nullius. The Aboriginals mistranslated this as Terror Nullius or, in their 834 languages, No Fear, so they kept rowing. Along the way they suffered more rifts, and some, including Eddie Mambo and his family, jumped out at the Thursday-to-Sunday Islands and Xmas Island, where they grew long white beards and pleasured themselves.

Being Gonads, the Aboriginals were rolling stones who gathered no moss. Instead they gathered Witchery grubs, sticks, stones, grass, beads and other oddments and condiments which they corroborated at their corroborees. Their most famous citizens were Bennelong, Manly, Wagga Wagga, Burnum Burnum & Bailey, Turramurra, North Turramurra, Dick A'Dick, King Billy and Jimmy Blacksmith.

They wore lioncloths around their lions. They were peaceful and happy and at One with Nature. They threw boomerangs at themselves, played the Didgeridoo-wop, and painted Dot-Matrix paintings which became very saleable in the New York art market. They buried each other in Scared Sights. Mostly, though, they slept and dreamed the Dreamtime, which went on for 40,000 years until they were woken up by the White Man, otherwise known as Whitie aka Paleface aka Moontan aka Casper the Unfriendly Ghost.

'Talking Points' for Reading Groups:
When the White Man arrived, why didn't

the Aboriginals tell him they'd baggsed it?
If not, do you think the White Men should
still have obeyed the Law of Baggsing?

2. The Second (Even Less Original) Australians

THE FIRST HONKY in Australia was an odorous Dutchman called Dirk Warthog. In defiance of the Terror Nullarbor policy, he landed in Western Australia. Seeing nothing there, he decided to leave. Before leaving he ate a meal on his special plate, which he then nailed to a tree. On the plate he carved the words 'Dirk Warthog was here'.

Hot on Dirk Warthog's wheels was the good Englishman William Damper, who found Warthog's plate nailed to the tree and cooked on it a new type of bread he invented and named after himself.

Chewing on his damper, Damper renamed the place New Holland in honour of the Dutch scum Dirk Warthog, who was the Hollandaise source. Having an English sense of humour, Dampener thought he could get a good laugh out of the old chaps in London when he went home and told them he'd called the driest, dustiest, most godforsakenest hellhole on earth (and elsewhere) after Holland. Tough cheddar!

Dampener nailed Dirk Warthog's plate back to the tree, where over time the lettering was to wear away until it caused great confusion to the explorers Don Berk and W.D. & H.O. Wills (see a later chapter but don't flick through too far or you'll spoil the ending).

Damper met some Aboriginals and asked to buy some of their Dot-Matrix paintings, which were hot in Soho. He offered some beads and trinkets and sly grog, but the Aboriginals said to their interpreter: 'Tell him he's Dreaming'. This was mistranslated to Damper as 'Sorry, we're Dreaming', so he went back to London Towne and said New Holland was ready to be invaded once the English had finished with Old Holland.

'Talking Points' for Reading Groups:
Why did Dutch and Portuguese explorers
come at all when they weren't English?

MESSER

He nailed the plate to a tree, where over time the lettering
was to wear away until it caused great confusion to the
explorers Don Berk and W.D. & H.O. Wills.

3. Captain Cook and His Bark Endeavour

Some histories have it that Captain Cook sailed a chook. These theories are now discredited. In fact he sailed a bark Endeavour, a much harder job than a chook given the porousness of his materials.

Cook followed another dirty Double-Dutch slimeball called Able Tasman, who missed the lush and fertile east coast of New Holland and went to New Zealand instead, which he found much more like Holland than Zealand until the Maoris ate him. This unfortunate setback ruined his chances of getting more famous, ie statues, *Who Weekly* covers etc.

On Captain Cook's bark ship, meanwhile, there was much pestilence and feculence. There was scurvy and rabies, and if Cook's semen got them both it was called scabies.

The only cure was lime cordigal and fruitbread, which was available in the South Sea Islands. On the way, Captain Cook, who was the first Australian to wear a curled wig in the mad manner of Totally Mad King George, discovered a great windswept bay which he named after his favourite subject, Botany.

Botany and Botany books were Cook's first love. He took with him the botanists Joseph Banks and Daniel Colander. Banks & Colander were the first of many great Australian men to travel in pairs (see Bass & Flinders, Don Berk and W.D. & H.O. Wills, Human Hovel, Flora & Fauna, Cobb & Co, Simpson & Donkey, Nock & Kirby, Lillee & Thomson etc).

Banks & Colander were never going to get too far. Banks would not be popular in Australia until the days of John 'Lawsy' Laws. And everyone found Colander such a strain. They were overtaken by another power couple, Bass & Flinders.

Bass & Flinders & their tomcat Tom sailed the *Trim Thumb* together down to Bass & Flinders Islands to find out what was happening down there. They discovered Flora & Fauna, which they drew in their Botany books, which they took back to Cook for marking. Cook was pleased with their work and with that of Colander. He named a fish after Bass & Flinders: the Bass.

They crossed the narrow and treacherous

waters south of Australia, which threw them thither and whither around the *Trim Thumb*. Bass (sometimes known as Balls) had a terrible time and lost his bearings, as all semen can do now and then. He discovered undiscovered longings and the love that dare not speak his name. Flinders eventually named the stretch of water in honour of his continuing valiant efforts to make Bass Straight.

Bass & Flinders discovered that Van Demon's Land was an island, by virtue of sailing around it. But then they broke up and Bass sailed to South America, where he was lost.

Flinders meanwhile married Ann Chappell in England and became the father of many fine cricketers. But he left her behind to sail *The Investigator* in the first circumcision of Australia. He was commemorated in all the places he circumstanced ie Flinders Street, Flinders Station, the Flinders Ranges, and In Flanders Fields where the poppies grow opium for export but for legitimate medical purposes only.

While Flinders was having all the adventures around the place, Captain Cook grew exhausted, and needed to go to Tahiti for a holiday and more fruitbread. 'Tahiti looks nice' were his famous last words to his first mate. 'Simon, Tahiti,' he said as they sailed the *Young Endeavour* off into the sunset.

There Cook met with the natives, who ate him uncooked with all his fruitbread and lime cordigal.

Moral for Focus Groups:
Plants have troubles, too.

MESSER

Captain Cook sailed a bark Endeavour.

4. The 1st Feet

MEANWHILE, BACK IN goode olde Englande there was a victimless crime problem. It was called victimless crime because there weren't any crimes or victims. Most of the people put in goals had stolen a loaf of bread to spend a penny. Nonetheless they were put in great ships on the Thames called Incredible Hulks.

There was much pestilence and feculence on the Incredible Hulks, particularly below decks, so the Department of Transportation decided to ship them all to the Great South Land instead. So everyone who stole a loaf of bread to spend a penny was sentenced to Public Transportation.

The 1st Feet of Incredible Hulks was captained by Phillip, who would be the 1st King of Australia. The main ships were the *Serious*, the *Possession with Intent to Supply*, and the *Bounty*.

Most of the convicts on board were pretty thieves and bawdy winches, but nonetheless much pestilence, feculence, petulance and flatulence prevailed below decks. There were many hardships and tallships. This was particularly so on the *Bounty*, which was captained by the wicked Captain Bligh.

Even when his men were dead of scurvy, rabies or scabies, Bligh would keelhaul them until they drowned. This led to a mutiny on the *Bounty* led by one of the better-dressed semen called Fletcher Jones. Fletcher Jones and his Mates (First, Second, Third, Fourth etc – they were all related) cast wicked Bligh adrift in a rowboat, and that was the last anyone saw of him.

Or was it???

Meanwhile Fletcher Jones and his well-dressed offshoots scuttled their butts to Pigpen Island where they had their wicked way with themselves and kept the British Umpire safe from the Enemy.

'Talking Points' for Reading Groups:
Why did they bring Bligh when he was
so hopeless?

Due to overcrowding, many convicts were kept on
Incredible Hulks on the River Thames.

5. The 1st Australia Day Celebrations

KING PHILLIP I and the rest of the 1st Feet made it to Sydney Cove just in time for that year's Australia Day honours. Phillip celebrated the day and found New South Wales. He so called it because it was south of Wales but not at all like Wales (he inherited Damper's funny olde Englishe sense of humour, for which they, the English, are world famous). He called it New to distinguish it from Old Sydney Town, or Olde Sydneye Towne as they called it backe thenne.

Wild times followed and much merriment. They drank from the Thanks Stream and had all their liquor on The Rocks and the first thing they built was a theatre-restaurant called Dirty Decks where the bawdy winches served ale. There was only one woman to go around every 40 or 50 men, so the women ended up being high-priced prostitutes. Desperately lacking low-priced call girls, the arrivals posted advertisements back in England saying 'Come to New South Wales, Ladies Get In Free'.

Phillip I, pure and honest as the day was long (or short, depending on the season), shunned the orgies and floggings of Olde Sydneye Towne, for he was most interested in the Aboriginals. Having been there for 40,000 years, most of the time Dreaming, the Aboriginals were very, very old. They were lucky the White Man had arrived to set up a colony because they were just about ready to die out of smallpox, alcohol, petrol-sniffing etc, not to mention very, very old age.

Luckily for them the White Men rescued the few survivors from their families and put them between the bosoms of the church.

Phillip's best friends were Bennelong and Manly, whom he discovered at either end of the Sydney Harbour ferry route. He loved to see Bennelong point to Manly. But Phillip's cruel friends also liked to get Bennelong drunk and dress him up in women's clothing for *The Footy Show*. Phillip saw Bennelong's cross-promotional potential and took him back to England, where he caught a fever and almost died of a broken heart. He returned home but caught a lurgy at Kissing Point, where he was known to frequent in his ladies' clothing with the Englishmen. Thus the reign of King Phillip I ended in tragedy.

The filthy French also tried to invade Australia in King Phillip's time, and bring their disgusting culture such as eating frogs, snails, puppydog's tails etc.

They were reputed to wash even less than the English. La Perouse arrived with Madame Tussaud to incite a French Revolution and rename the colony New South Quebec. They landed coincidentally at La Perouse where, finding Australia already invaded by Aboriginals and Englishmen on the grog, they had little to do.

Moral for Focus Groups:
Curiosity killed the captain.

6. A Succession of Unknown Kings

FOLLOWING KING PHILLIP were King John Hunter, Philip Giggly King and another unknown King who has fallen out of memory.

King John Hunter was a stern man who named things after himself then went home. King King named the few things that were left after himself and went home too. The other man, Lieutenant Governor, also named a certain number of things after himself.

The real power in the colony was John Macarthur, who had a farm at Parramatta called Macarthur Park. He had any number of sheep there, and entertained himself by riding on the sheep's back. Soon he got the whole of the country doing so for his pleasure.

They drank a lot of rum and sang songs, such as 'Yo Ho Ho and a Bottle of Rum', then the national anthem, and 'Old Macarthur Had a Farm'.

The indiscipline in the colonies sent Totally Mad King George even Madder than he was already, so he sent wicked old Bligh to set things straight. Bligh had gone to fat since his early days in *Mutiny on the Bounty*, and now lived as a recluse in the South Sea Islands and charged a million dollars per movie. He was still terrified of Fletcher Jones. When he got to New South Wales, he took all the rum away from Macarthur Park and hid it under his bed.

This bold move triggered the Rum Rebellion. Singing 'Yo Ho Ho and a Bottle of Rum' was markedly less amusing when all the rum had been hidden.

Macarthur formed the Rum Core, whose mission was to find out where all the rum had gone. After they'd searched everywhere else, they went to Government House, and finally to Bligh's bedroom. Seeing nothing there, they were set to leave. Just then someone heard a sucking sound. They tore up the bed to find Bligh in his nightshirt trying to finish the last of their rum.

So for the second time in his life Bligh was mutinied. He fled to the South Sea Islands and lived with Fletcher Jones's descendants, only surfacing briefly for extortionate appearance fees.

Moral for Focus Groups:
Lie down with fleece, wake up with dags.

John Hunter was a stern man who named things after himself then went home.

7. Macquarie and Macarthur – a Scotsman

MACQUARIE WAS THE canny Scotsman who was sent to Sort Everything Out. He did so by introducing Scotch instead of Rum'n'Raisins, which put the Rum Core out of business. The Scotch Core wore kilts and played with their bagpipes, which confused everybody, including Old Macarthur, who licked his wounds out at Macarthur Park.

Historians tend to confuse Macarthur and Macquarie. They were no friends. In fact, they were never seen in the same room together, and never appeared on the same money together, giving rise to the theory that Macarthur and Macquarie were in fact . . . the SAME MAN!

This theory was reinforced by the fact that Macquarie built a chair for his wife in the Botanical Gardens, but it was Macarthur's wife, Elizabeth, who was much more famous and sat there.

Macquarie/Macarthur emaciated the convicts and built many monuments. His chief architect was Peter Greenaway, who had stolen a loaf of bread and was sentenced to Public Transportation with the cook, the thief, his wife and her lover.

Macquarie/Macarthur emaciated Greenaway and set him to hugh sandstone. Greenaway's great achievements were the Town Hall, Parliament House, the Law Courts, St James's Church, St Paul's Cathedral, the Great Synagogue, the Opera House, Government House, the Harbour Bridge South Pylon, the Kremlin, The Rocks etc. He died a pauper.

The English did not like Macquarie, so they sent out Mr Big to keep an eye on him. Macquarie, who had much to hide, got jack of this so he decided to go back home to Bonnie Scotland. When Macquarie left town in 1815, he confirmed the suspicion that he was Macarthur by gazing back fondly on the Botanical Gardens and saying 'I misses Macquarie's chair'.

Suspiciously, from the day Macquarie left Sydney, Macarthur was never seen again but his last words would ring in memory:

'I Will Returf.'

'Talking Points' for Reading Groups:
What does a Scotchman wear under his quilt?

His chief architect was Peter Greenaway, who had stolen a loaf of bread and was sentenced to Public Transportation.

Mix'n'Match Quiz:
The Early Times

These explorers said these things. See if you can match them up:

1. 'The miserableblest people in the world'.
2. 'There was no good to be done there'.
3. 'Land ho'.
4. 'Dr Livingstone I presume'.

A. Damper.
B. Jansz.
C. Cook.
D. Stanley Knife.

Emaciated convicts got:

a. Ticket of leave.
b. Female Factory.
c. 40 lashings.
d. Boils.

What was hardest to get in Olde Sydneye Towne?

    a. TB.

    b. TV.

    c. VD.

    d. VB.

Who was Macquarie's biggest enemy?

    a. Bent.

    b. Bigge.

    c. Mort.

    d. Nun.

8. The Age of the Explorers: 37, 44, 52, 44, 35, 29 and 41

THE 1ST EXPLORERS were of course Blaxland, Lawson and Wentworth Falls, or alternatively, Blaxland, Wentworth and Lawson. They were known as the 3 Sisters.

Billy Wentworth Falls was a venereal politician who was later to find the Constitution and Grey Power. He was notable for his high stiff collars which he wore even while exploring. Lawson was a poet who wrote 'The Man from Snowy River' while discovering the Blue Mountains. Blaxland was simply Blaxland.

They followed the train line up the Blue Mountains and named suburbs after themselves. When they reached the 3 Sisters lookout they saw more Blue Mountains but no sheep.

The 1st explorers were lucky, as 1st explorers go, because they had a road to follow. This road had been built by John Oxley, who was not an explorer but an emaciated convict whose steady working habits as a member of road gangs, chain gangs, streets gangs etc had equipped him well for the task.

Governor Lachlan Macquarie had sent Oxley to search for the Inland Sea or alternatively for green pastures to braise sheep. Oxley built Oxley's Road over the Blue Mountains but he only found more trees, no sea or pastures. He also saw rivers, which he named the Lachlan and the Macquarie, although some believe he actually named them the John and the Oxley but unknown persons changed them when he got home.

Oxley's handmade road over the Blue Mountains thus waived the pay for Blaxland, Lawson and Wentworth who being a threesome and three's a crowd could never agree and kept wandering off the track. Their path was to become the world-famous Zigger Zagger Railway.

They went in search of Dirk Warthog's tree and found it closer than it had been. They named it The Explorer's Tree in honour of Damper. Then they turned around and went home to Olde Sydneye Towne, which was about to move to Gosforde, because Wentworth had to find the Constitution and be a politician, Lawson had many poems and books to write, and Blaxland had to go on being Blaxland.

The 2nd explorer was Leichhardt, the first man to discover that going to Queensland in search of a good caffè latte is not a good idea. He'd been looking for Balmain, but once Leichhardt got onto Oxley's Road there were no U-turns allowed and before he knew it he was lost in Queensland.

There were many other explorers who went in search of the Inland Sea and new pastures for braising sheep. They got lost near Mount Disappointment and Desolation Hill, so they should have known.

'Talking Points' for Reading Groups:
Who explored the most, as in,
who came first?
If ants were people, they could walk around the world in a day. Think about that for 30 seconds, please.

9. Human Hovel: A Great Australian

THE NEXT MAIN explorer was Human Hovel. Earlier explorers had been looking for Inland Seas and pastures to braise sheep, but now the explorers were all looking for the earlier explorers who'd got lost, eg Leichhardt.

Human Hovel was a keen explorer even as a child, when he chopped down a cherry tree and discovered new land at Berrima. The new Governor, Brisvegas, sent Human Hovel out to find Leichhardt but he took a left turn at Woodville Road and instead followed the Hume Highway down south. In a long trip, Human Hovel crossed the Snowy Mountains (where he should have realised he was a long way from Brissie) and ended up in Melbourne on a Mystery Flight.

Things got desperate, so Human Hovel ate his bullocks and his boots and his books and finally fish. He invented a new form of house to shelter from the snow and rain in Melbourne. He named it after himself: the Human Hovel.

When Human Hovel got home, the new

Governor, Darling, pointed Charles Sturt to the Inland Sea where Leichhardt had last been seen headed. Taking Human Hovel with him, Sturt followed Oxley's Road and the Lachlan Macquarie Rivers until he discovered Aboriginals, whom Sturt called 'a merry people and sit up laughing and talking more than half of the night'.

Sturt and Human Hovel soon got sick of the Aboriginals keeping them awake all night so they kept walking. Tired from their sleepless nights, they squabbled and went in indifferent directions. Human Hovel went home to his farm. Sturt lost track of Leichhardt but found the Murray River and boarded a houseboat and sailed to South Australia. On his way back he got lost in the desert and ran out of food and water and caught scurvymungus. He created water for himself by peeing into a solar still. And so he didn't find the Inland Sea, but he became famous for the invention of Sturt's Desert Pee.

From the Desk of Mr Slack:
Don't sit up laughing all night, go to bed!

FAQs on Part 1*

Which was the bit where the least happened, so we know to gloss it over?

If I could choose between Australian history and English or American or Russian or Chinese or even Irish, why would I choose to have Australian?

I am a parent of young children. Is Australian history rated G, PG, M or R?

If we were to discuss Australian history over dinner, which course would you advise?

What if someone asks us something?

[*Unfortunately, due to a high traffic of calls at this stage, we have no FAAs to our FAQs. You have been placed in a Q and will be attended to shortly. Please mail suggestions to Mr Slack or better still stop A-ing so many F-ing Qs.]

Part 2

the BORING TIMES

Then came the first of the Boring Times when there was No Australian History. Australian History is world famous for its Boring Times. We had to rely on Imported Products such as the French Revelation, the American Civil Wart, Ratio Nelson and The Battle Of Trafalgar Square, Neapolitan and Waterloo, and the Merchant—Ovary dramas.

[Note: Some historians say this was the first of the Exciting Times when there was Much Australian History. These historians are thought to be featherbedding their own nests, ie creating business for themselves. Why we need these mass debates going on forever is beyond us and UnAustralian and typical of the Elites.]

Australian History suffered badly through lack of it. There were few memorable governors and even fewer of the governed. This state of affairs lasted through the Hungry Forties until the Roaring Nineties. But it was then that the people became institutionalised.

10. Pasteurising the Land

FOLLOWING MACARTHUR, EVERYONE jumped aboard the sheep's back and rode it till it hurt. Clip went the shears, boys, clip! clip! clip! The young colony was a land of muscle men in blue singlets with their wide and narrow combs, and the sheep they loved. We supplied Olde Englande with all the woolly jumpers and tea cosies and leg warmers they needed for their frosty winters.

Most of the Australian lands were still virgins, so they were squatted on by squatters. Most squatters were filthy hippies and ferals who wanted to get out of paying rent, but many raised and shore up their own sheep and so before long they grew wealthy and became a squattocracy. They went to the toilet crouching down and thus they pasteurised the land.

Moral for Focus Groups:
He who hesitates got lost.

MESSER

Australia's early landholders were known as 'squatters'.

11. Batman and Melbourne

BATMAN WAS AUSTRALIA'S first superhero. He went down south to Port Phillip Bay and met with the Aboriginals who lived there. The Aboriginals were the bain-marie of the White Man's existence, spoiling his pasteurised lambs and wrestling his sheep. So Batman gave them tomahawks, trinkets, odds and sods, gold, frankincense and myrrh, in exchange for Melbourne. Knowing how the weather is there, the Aboriginals figured they had a bargain. But others, like Said Hanrahan, were more doubtful. They said Batman was robbin' the black man and we'll all be rooned.

But there were even more serious problems for Bantam. The colonial powers that been said, 'If you give Aboriginals tomahawks etc for their land, then they'll want a whole lot more tomahawks for the rest of the continent we've already taken, and we don't have enough tomahawks to make good on the deal.'

The powers that been wanted to cancel the

treatises Bantam had made. But it was too late. Thousands of free settlers and free squatters had moved down to Melbourne riding on the sheep's back, and before you could say 'fee fi fo fum' the Englishman had pasteurised all the lands Batman had been robbin' off the black fellow. They put their sheep there and they grew Australian Wools, which became very popular in Melbourne and a new religion.

'Talking Points' for Reading Groups: How much myrrh would you swap for Melbourne these days (taking inflation into account)?

Batman gave the Aboriginals trinkets, odds and sods, frankincense and myrrh in exchange for Melbourne.

12. Gold!

'THERE'S GOLD IN them thar hills!'
And so it began.

The Gold Rushes were the most exciting times in olden times except for the Bull Rushes and the Bum's Rushes and the Last-Minute Rushes. The Gold Rushes were all about 'nuggets', ie golden, black, chicken etc.

The first nugget was discovered by Johnny Hargreaves, which led to the invention of Chinese food and other benefits like Democracy. The first biggest nugget was the Gold Standard, which brought bounty hunters running into the rivers with their pots 'n' pans 'n' other inventions such as the cat's cradle, the spinning jenny, the klondike etc.

The first Golf Rush was in California, off the east coast of New South Wales. The local Australian authorities didn't want the news to get out, because if there was a golf rush there might be no-one left in the cities to clean out the toilets, collect garbage, brush the Governor's boots, sit in the Legislative Council etc.

Johnny Hargreaves went to Californ-I-A with his three mates: John Lister and the Tom Brothers, Henry and Tom. They didn't find any gold but they brought back the latest trends from the USA, which meant everyone followed them out to O'Fear near Bathurst with their pots 'n' pans. Sure enough, Hargreaves found his big nugget and told the world, which meant Lister and Henry Tom and Tom Tom got nothing. Do you think that was fair?

Batman's colony down in Melbourne started to empty out as men rushed up to Bathurst. Soon there was no-one left. So to get people back to Victoria the tourism commission put up a big reward for anyone whoever should find golf in Ballarat or Bendigo.

They always had to put up incentives to stop people leaving Victoria, due to the climate.

But lo and behold, they found even bigger nuggets in Victoria than they found in Bathurst, and soon there was no-one left in O'Fear, they were all south of the boarder.

Golf fever swept the nation, and everyone downed tools in the cities and travelled on male coaches to the Diggings, where they became

Diggers. Police and sailors quit their postings and ran to the gold fields. Fathers desserted their families in the hope of making them rich. Children were abandoned in their cots while their parents went off and gambled and hoped to become rich desserters. Men's eyes spun round and round with hope for fool's gold.

When they got to the gold fields, most of these men discovered golf but drank it away.

Golf mining towns were successful places because everyone left the fetid gritty air of the dusty dirty city and headed for the gold fields, where they built new fetid gritty cities. They had barber shops, banks and bawdy houses. Everyone was happy except the Diggers who died in their Diggings and the Drinkers who died in their Drinkings.

'Talking Points' for Reading Groups:
Did they have high minds, or were the gold diggers just bloody gold diggers?

13. The Eureka Stockyard

THE SOUTHERN CROSS is the flag bikie gangs and Confederates and Republicans have worn ever since the Civil War. It started when a Digger was murdered in the Diggings and the Paris Commune spread around the world.

The Diggers wanted Democracy, the Confederates wanted slavery, the Communards wanted communism, the bikies wanted to ride without helmets, the women wanted Universal Suffering, everyone wanted rites etc, and this all came to a head when a Digger named Peter Labor fell in the bath and said 'Eureka!'

What followed is still uncertain. Diggers burned their driver's licences and 1,000 of them moved into a Stockyard. Many of them went home again when they got hungry, and because Australian men don't want to fight the police especially when it comes to protecting their rites.

What was left in the Stockyard was the Irish, who were too thick and drunk being bog Irish to go home. They flew the Southern Cross

Confederate Flag proudly over their heads. There was talk of a referendum on the republic.

The next morning the police came and killed them all, except for Peter Labor, who had his arm amputated due to a septic shank.

Therefore the Eureka Stockyard was a great victory for the working class and we celebrate it still on Anzac Day.

Moral for Focus Groups:
Don't die with the music in your pocket.

14. Democracy

IN THE BORING Times many people became well known who were to get their pictures onto $5, $10, $20 etc notes. One was Caroline Chisel, about whom nothing is known. She was on the $5 note for a while. She was a poor but honest girl who needed the helpy. She arrived in Australia in 1838 as a Boat People Person and took seedy girls off the streets where they were working and gave them a home.

Her homes were filled with rats, which she killed by feeding them lace breaded with arsenic. She helped migrants, the unemployed, single mothers, the disabled and other dole bludgers. As a result she died penniless and forgotten.

Brisvegas was Governor for many years and then became a city in Queensland. Governor Brisvegas also became a river, as did Darling, another of the Boring Governors.

Australia was still not civilised or multicultural. It was impossible to get good Thai or Mexican food or find a working public telephone (they

Caroline Chisel was a poor but honest girl who needed the helpy.

didn't have mobiles yet). Our main contribution to humanity so far was to expand the world's known resources of real estate. Soon someone realised we had to have Democracy, which was all the rage in America, France etc.

Democracy came in two parts: You had to have Government that was Responsible, and Representative. Nobody knew what this meant, but they were paying taxes for Irresponsible and Unrepresentative Government so the popular slogans of the time were 'Liberty, Equality, and Fraternity Houses!' and 'No Taxation Without Sensation!'

So we got a mixture of Responsible and Representative Government, known as Reprehensible Government.

Reprehensible Government divided the country into seats. Each seat was divided into wards of the state. Wards were divided into booths. In every booth was a pencil. And for the first time anywhere in the world, you could go into a booth with a pencil and do your Secret Ballet. This was called an Election.

The Secret Ballet elected an Upper House and a Lower House, though to confuse the enemy they were both housed within the same House on the same floor and the Lower House was more important because it was the People's House while the Upper House was someone else's, but whose exactly was never made clear.

The squatters campaigned for their own House in which they would squat. But nobody else wanted this, and some called it a Bunyip Aristocracy, which got it laughed out of court because it was so funny.

Imagine an aristocracy of bunyips!

Things were too exciting for words!

Women campaigned for Universal Suffering, and they got it – we were the first country in the world!

This was called the Axminster System. As Australians, it is our proudest system!

From the Desk of Mr Slack:
Write it down on paper or else!

MESSER

For the first time anywhere in the world, you could go into
a booth and do your Secret Ballet.

15. Don Berk and
W.D. & H.O. Wills

THE LAST EXPLORERS to head west in search of Leichhardt were Donald O'Hara Berk and W.D. & H.O. Wills. Don Berk was a wild bog Irishman who had fought for England (versus Ireland), Ireland (versus England), Brussels (versus no-one) and the Hungarian Hussies (opponent TBA). His favourite activities were dancing, womenising, duelling, gambling on poker machines, and of course fighting.

Berk came to Australia in the Golf Rush, but there was no gold left so he became a copper which was cheaper and better paid. He was notorious for rattling magistrates' gates and bathing stark naked in puddles of rainwater, clad in nothing but his police helmet and a good book.

He wrote notes all over the walls of his house and one said 'You are requested not to read anything on the walls!', which convinced all who knew him that he was mad as a coot and should be sent a long way away asap.

Berk fell in love with an opera singer named

Wendy Matthews and pretended to travel around as a policeman when he was really following her from show to show. He asked her for her hand but she gave him a glove. It is said he often dribbled spit into his long beard, but on this day he dribbled tears.

In 1860 Berk and his friend W.D. & H.O. Wills were asked to go north young man, just keep going and see what is there, and, if any luck, Leichhardt. They rode camels which were led by the nose and their trusty sidekick, who was Joe King. They left Olde Sydneye Towne to a great procession of cheering crowds.

They went to the Golf of Cafeteria and never quite saw the water (or Leichhardt) but still saw a lot of marshes. Near enough was good enough, so they turned around. Theirs was an epic journey and they soon became thirsty. Their camels were shits of the desert but Berk got so hungry he ate them, and still he had not found Leichhardt.

Berk and W.D. & H.O. Wills came to the Red Centre, where they discovered the Explorer's Tree left by Blaxland, Lawson and Wentworth Falls. This was also the tree found by Dirt Warthog back in the earliest days. The lettering on Dirt Warthog's plate had worn off, leaving only the letters D, I and G.

Obeying the command of the Explorer's Tree, Berk and W.D. & H.O. Wills ordered Joe King to dig until he made it to china. There was some dirty old crockery under the tree, but no china. They came to Coopers Creek but their back-up team had left nine hours earlier, so they kept on walking into the desert. Tragically, they were betrayed by the DIG tree and for reasons unknown that will forever remain a mystery, Berk and W.D. & H.O. Wills were lost in the dessert.

The only survivor was the faithful Joe King, who led the camels back to water and made them drink, what's more. When Joe King got to Sydney, the first man he met was another explorer heading out of town.

'Living stoned, I presume,' said King.

'You must be Joe King,' said the other man.

After this tragedy, it was decided that enough had been discovered of the Red Centre and there would be no more tragic explorers until small planes and helicopters made the journey easier.

Bush Survival Tip for Focus Groups:
Dogs can dig quicker in sand.

16. The Park Rangers

Everybody's favourite Australian Heroes are the Park Rangers, such as Bennie Hall, Captain Morgan, Ned Kelly, Jessie James, Cobb & Co, Thunderbolt & Lightfoot, Moonlite and Starlite. Once upon a time their faces appeared on the notes of the money they stole. Hence they were known as 'Currency Lads'.

The best Park Rangers were Frank Gardener and his gang, which included Bennie Hall and Eddie Gilbert. They robbed the coaches carrying gold from the coal mines. They would bail them out with shot guns and then retire to the pubs where they shot glasses.

Frank Gardener was also known as Frank Clarke, Darkie Gardener, Frank Smith, Frank Jones and the Very Reverend Frank Christie. After retiring very wealthy as a Park Ranger, he went to California where he established a saloon bar and died peacefully from pneumonia, although he may have died unpeacefully from being shot in a card game.

Gardener's faithful follower was Bennie Hall, who was known as Brave Ben. Bennie was a stockman who had bad luck with women. He married Bridget Jones and they set up a property at Sandy Creek until she ran away with John Taylor, a vicious bent copper. Bennie was angry so he got arrested for robbery of underarms, a stunt he pulled at the race track. When he went home his land was depredated so he fell in with Gardener's gang and they became proper professional Park Rangers, very good judges of horse flesh.

When Gardener went to California Bennie Hall became the leader of the band and was generally victimised because of the victim mentality. He stole Bathurst and much mail – the Park Rangers were pranksters who stole a lot of mail – with 600 robberies in all. He never killed anyone so it was an injustice when he was shot in the back by troopers who peppered him with shot grapes.

Captain Morgan and Captain Moonlite and Captain Thunderbolt and Captain Beefheart were all the same rank so they worked separately in order to escape demarcation disputes.

The best one was Captain Thunderbolt, who was in and out of goal for horse-wrestling. He stuck up people who were stuck up and robbed them blindly. He would help himself to their prize beasts. He had a faithful sidekick whose name was Yellow Long, aka Yellilong, aka Mary Ann Bugg. She even brought her children with her when she rode with Captain Thunderbolt.

Thunderbolt was chased by police up to Urethra, near Armidale. He had a drinke at the inne, whereafter he was surrounded by Trooper Walker. They had an excellent gunfight until Walker chased Thunderbolt into a river and shot his chest out. Walker dragged him up to the bank . . . but Thunderbolt was DEAD!

Captain Starlite and Captain Moonlite and Captain Beefheart were also into robbery of underarms. But they were very very wronged. It was generally the police's fault, for none of them were Captains, they were bent coppers, and who remembers the names of any of the police involved?

It is always the Park Rangers we shall remember, lest we forget. Moonlite/Starlite was a lay-down misere preacher who was said to have fought in the Italian civil war, he so hated Italians. Then he came out and robbed a lot of mailmen and bank tellers in the usual way and was sent to goal. After his release he hit the celebrity speakers' circuit until he got bored and went back on the road, robbing underarms with great charm. Along the way he killed a corrupt cop who deserved it, but Moonlite was hanged until he was dead in goal, which was also the end of his public speaking career. Like all Park Rangers, he was a legend.

'Talking Points' for Reading Groups:
If you could be a Park Ranger or a bent copper, which would you be?
Which Park Ranger was the best?

Captain Thunderbolt stuck up people who were stuck up
and robbed them blindly.

17. Ned Kelly: He Robbed the Rich and Stole from the Poor

B UT THE KING of the Park Rangers was 'Ned' Kelly, a Bog Irishman who liberated Australia from the tyranny of distance.

Kelly was a wild colonial boy of poor but honest parents he was born in Castlemaine XXXX. His family were persecuted by the English with their persecution complex. There resulted a Potato Famine which brought the Bog Irish out of their Bogs and their hero was young 'Red Ned' Kelly.

Kelly robbed the rich and stole from the poor. He won the bloody battles of Eureka Stockyard, the Gold Rush, Culloden, the Alamo, Rorke's Drift, Gallipoli etc. He collected his Chain Gang of Park Rangers around him who included his very brother Dan Kelly, Frank Burns and Brave Heart, and they went on a ramraid killing policemen although some reports say the policemen killed them.

Kelly had many grievances including a beard. His mother, known as 'Mrs' Kelly, was thrown

into goal for stealing a loaf of bread and trans-
portated thus. 'Ned' Kelly hustled horses and
buggered sheep but that was regular for his life &
times. He was a friend of the Aboriginals and
signed land rights treaties with them. He was also
totally into the environment etc.

'Ned' Kelly had many pen pals around the
world and his favourite pastime apart from
wrestling horses and getting shot by policemen
was to write letters. He and his Chain Gang
liberated the Australia Post Office in Jerryderry
and there 'Ned' sat down to write his famous
Londonderry Letter which was a chain letter
raising moneys for his Gang and the liberation of
all impressed peoples around the world ie the
Irish, Aboriginals etc.

There he fell in love with Maid Marilyn but her
whereabouts were unknown.

The Kelly Chain Gang were betrayed by Aaron
Sheriff their old friend and they were framed for
bloody killing him.

'Ned' had a dream to post his letters on a train
so next he liberated the Australia Post Office at
Garryowen. He wore an Australia Post letterbox
on his head and looked upon the world through
its slot.

MESSER

Ned Kelly had many grievances, including a beard.

His Chain Gang also wore letterboxes and the milk churns that country people turn into letterboxes. They told jokes and composed bush ballads in the Garryowen P.O. which was then burned down by arseholists.

'Ned' wore chain mail and sent chain mail.

Finally the police led by the wicked Governor Bligh arrived for Kelly's bloody Last Stand. He derailed the mail train wearing his letterbox and shot all the police and cried: 'I am the bloody library monitor!'

They shot him and then took him from that place to another place and then to yet another place where he was hanged until he be dead by the Hanging Judge whose name was Barry.

And that was the legend of 'Red Ned' Kelly. He was later painted as a blockhead and starred in several movies, music videos etc.

Moral for Focus Groups:
If you lose your horses you go mad.

18. Queensland: the Queens' Land

SOMETIME THEREAFTER THE Founding Fathers decided New South Wales was getting too big, so they invented Queensland to the north. Queensland would be different, they decided. No more death duties or welfare cheats or dole bludgers, no arts wankers, no caffè latte, no girls, no Aboriginals or anything. What they would have was lots of sweet things ie sarsaparilla, ginger, sugar cane, pineapples, bananas etc.

To harvest the pineapples, bananas and sugar they brought in slave labourers from the South Sea Islands. These slaves were called Kayaks. Many thousands of the Kayaks were stolen by slave ship captains (including Bligh) and were keelhauled into Queensland.

Their leader was Kunta Kintay, and their story is told in *Roots*. But soon the poor white trash in the Queensland cities got jealous of all the work the Kayaks were getting, while they themselves got none, and soon the law was passed to give more money and houses to the urban poor white trash so they could sit in their Queenslanders and drink XXX beer, while taking money away from the Kayaks, who already had nothing, so it was a great economic miracle up there.

**Morals for Focus Groups:
None in Queensland.**

Part 3

Australia the YOUNG NATION

In the Third Part of Australian history, Australia became Australia at long last. The nation was found by Sir Henry National Parkes, who had a mighty beard. Once we had a nation and Pryministers and a Capital, we needed to prove something to ourselves so we went to war, against the Bores first but then against the Germans who were also Bores. We proved ourselves the best in the world at laying down our lives for the British Umpire.

We also proved ourselves the best at tragic heroes such as Name Belly Delta, Far Lap's Heart, Less Darcy and Sir Donald Bradperson. We were prouder of them than we were of our politicians, who included Red Ted Theodore, Sir Jack Lang, Billy-Bob Hughes, Curtain/ Chifley and Pig-Eye Bob Menzies, and they were all scoundrels as you would expect, especially Bug-Eyes McMahon. But somehow the Young Nation pulled through and became a Middle-Aged Nation by the Fifties.

19. Federation: Discuss

THE FATHER OF FEDERATION was Henry National Parkes. He stood on a mountain with his tablets and made a speech known as the Tenterfield Saddler, which began 'Four Score and Ten Years Ago'. We were tired of living under the yolk of Britain, so we had a war of incontinence between the red coats and the blue coats which ended with one side winning.

The Founding Fathers, such as Henry National Parkes, Billy Wentworth, Victor Trumper, Don Bradperson and Mulga Bill, wrote our morning constitutional, which gave us the Fifth Amendment and the national anthem. Doing a constitutional was not easy work, so the Founding Fathers left it all unclear. The Privet Council remained important.

What Federation really meant was that New South Wales was not a colony anymore, it was a nation, called 'Australia'. Victoria, Queensland and the other parts of the compass remained colonies of New South Wales.

Federation finally occurred in 1901. It was Sir Henry National Parkes's finest moment albeit he had died in 1896.

We celebrate Federation every year on New Year's Eve.

From the Desk of Mr Slack:
Make sure you can spell it before you do it!

20. The Tomb of the Unknown Pryministers

THE FIRST AUSTRALIAN Pryministers are unknown. Their names were Barton Fink, Bobby Fisher, Deacon Deakin, Red Hill, Gladstone, Disraeli, Emerson, Lake and Palmer.

Why were they unknown? We may never know. Some historians say it was because they put the capital in Canberra, where they had to live because they had their own personalised suburbs: Barton, Forrest, Deakin, Fisher, Kingston and Red Hill. But Canberra was the miserablest place on earth and there was nothing there, so when the Pryministers disappeared to Canberra nothing was heard from them again.

Most is known about Deacon Deakin, who was known as Affable Alfred. Deakin wrote poetry, so he became a politician. He had a deep rich voice and spoke down to people with it. He improved their conditions etc and invented the old age pensioner.

Deakin became Pryminister three different times. Each time it was the wrong time, so he quit or was sacked so he could come back when the time suited him better. In his first speech to the parliament, he used the opportunity to resign. Sometimes he wrote newspaper articles under a pseudo name in which he criticised his own actions?! Deacon Deakin or Affable Alfred was one mixed-up mofo. He was like a heavyweight champion who keeps getting beaten up but they can't keep him down and if they don't knock him down he'll knock himself down, himself.

It is unknown why or indeed where or, in fact, who were the full list of early Pryministers. But their contribution to our great story cannot be misunderestimated. They found the nation and had parties such as Labor and Wig Protection. They are unremembered on any of our money but they were very into protection rackets and free trade. But most importantly, they forged the Young Nation by sending us to . . . War.

From the Desk of Mr Slack:
Shut your eyes NOW and see if you can
remember any! No peeking!

meet ur 4bears
(or: What if some great Aussies sent text messages from Beyond the Grave?)

Dame St Mary Mackillop: Our 1st St

hi im m mck & I begat 2 miracles.
im eldest of 8 chn . . . a poor but honest
farmer i was born in castle cove.
i was swf, wkd as au pair & babysitter 4 poor
ppl coz 0 children had any school 2 go 2.
w/ cazza chisel & dame gary gilmore & other
womyn on dollar notes (but not the queen), i
wkd 4 free then Bcame poor & ate humble
pie.
my miracle was the oafs & the fishes.
2Bcome a saint i had 2 perform 1other
miracle – 2 strikes & ur in!!!
i set 2 work on this <holy order> & B4 long
did it by raising Glenn Lazarus from tha
dead.
i was very popular, 2.
ps in case ur wondring heavens not all it wuz
crackd up 2B . . . 2many bloody nuns!!!!!

21. Bongo Paterson's Curse

BONGO PATERSON WAS introduced into the colony at an early age. He lived in the dusty dirty city with the air so fowl and gritty, and wished he could go droving down the Lachlan so we don't know where he are. He camped by a billabong under the shane of a cooler bark tree, and sang a jolly jumbuck one two three.

He went to town for a shave and came out looking like the man from Iron Bru, but from there on it was all overflow, until the cold from old Regretel Packer got away and we don't know where she are.

It was a very confusing life, as you will appreciate, and became more so when people started calling him after a ukelele. He played songs and wrote rhymes for the *Bullet Tin*, which was a famous magazine that had gossip about Australian celebrities in it instead of English, so it was very important in its way in its day and Bongo became its biggest name.

He went to the war and participated in the

charge of the Light Horse Brigade against the Germans, and won. He came home and wrote a poem about it called 'The Man from Snowy River'. And that was, as they say in literature, The End.

'Talking Points' for Reading Groups: Bloody elites!

22. Mawson of the Atlantic

SIR DOUGLAS MAWSON was another of our great banknotes. He was known as the 'grey nurse'.

A native of Rooty Hill, Mawson explored the Atlantic with Shackleton, an explorer from England played by Sir Kenneth Branagh. Mawson climbed Mount Erebus air disaster and founded the Mawson Island Fig, which was a fruit.

He slid off the South Pole with his huskies and circumambulated Atlantica. Most of his team and huskies were never seen again, that is how long it took.

He got home with frostbite and the subtraction of certain toes. But that did not deter him. He went back to the Atlantic Circle and discovered much more of it, claiming it all as Australian Capital Territory.

When he died Mawson became a famous station.

Survival Tip for Focus Groups:
Pack the night before.

23. Name Belly Delta

TAME DELLY MELBA was named after a peach dish and became a world-famous opera. She began her music career when her father promised her a gold watch if she could play twelve pieces on his organ. He was an orgiast at a church.

When she finished school she wanted to become an opera so she studied under Petrocelli in Munich and married Louis Armstrong. As a human being she was said to be a total prima donna.

Her first name was not Dame Melly Thelma. It was Margaret Mitchell. But an operatic must have a stage name or pseudo name, and once she took one of these she became a huge hit with top forty songs and everything. She took Europe by storm!

The interesting thing about her is that she faked her death. Every time she pretended to die, she came back soon afterwards. She kept on doing it until it was like the little Girl who cried 'Wolf!' and by the end nobody believed her anymore.

She died penniless and alone.

Serving Suggestion for Reading Groups:
If you sing for your supper, make sure it's still hot.

24. The Bore Wore

THE NEW YOUNG Nation needed a war to defend itself. We had many threats: the Yellow Peril, the Green Hornet, the Black Prince, the Brown Snake etc. As a new Young Nation we were surrounded on all sides with Boat People and our poorest boarders were no good for keeping all the threats out.

The biggest threats of all were the Bores. We had Bores all over the countryside for drinking water. But the biggest Boors of all were in South Africa. So our young and proud and free nation forged itself in war, and defended itself by going to South Africa and killing them all in the Bore Wore.

The greatest hero of the Bore Wore was Breaker Breaker. He led the troops in the charge and said: 'Shoot straight you bastards!' so they wouldn't miss the Boars.

Breaker Breaker was a fine hoarse man who could ride bare back in bib and braces. He was also a dab hand on Mulga Bill's bicycle, which

was a penny farting and therefore the most diffi-
cult of all. He was a colourful character, all right.
He married Daisy Bates and several others at the
same time.

The Queen at the time was Victoria. With his
ripe language, Breaker Breaker made Victoria
cross. So the bastards shot him instead.

Meanwhile the Boars and the British were all
eaten by Zulus at Dorke's Rift, so in the end, the
Zulus came first, Australia probably second, the
British third, and the Boors last. Though historians are still checking those results.

Moral for Focus Groups:
Death can be fatal.

With his ripe language, Breaker Breaker made
Victoria cross.

25. The Anzac Biscuit Legend

WHEN THE WAR to End All Warts broke out, Australia rushed off to defend our umpire. Winston Dunhill was in charge of the British Navy, and he identified the soft underbelly of the Turkey. This was a place known as Gulliboli.

Gulliboli was a great military victory for Australia. Our boys fought on the beaches, in the trenches, on the landing grounds etc, as Dunhill said, and they charged at Johnny Turk with their castanets fixed.

Johnny Turk was a Muslin, so of course he was a gutless woman-hating hashish-smoker and ran away, which is what all Muslins do.

Australia took over Gulliboli and celebrated Anzac Day which was the end of the War to End All Warts. The heroes were Mel Gibson and the blond guy who did nothing after this. They cooked oatmeal cookies which became known as Anzac Biscuits, in honour of biscuits.

From then on, Australia celebrates all her great

victories on Prozac Day, when we say: 'Let's Re Forget', which is Latin.

Handy Household Tip for Focus Groups:
Look before you leak.

Australia celebrates all great victories on Prozac Day.

26. Bobby Simpson and his Donkey

O F ALL THE great legends to come out of our great warts, the greatest was Bobby Simpson and his Donkey. Simpson – alias Simpson Kirkpatrick, aka Simpson Kilpatrick, aka Oysters Kilpatrick, aka Oysters Natural, aka Au Naturel, aka Au Revoir – was, you guessed it, fighting in France. He had a donkey on which he led his wife Florence Nightingale who was with child to a mangy, left them there, and went out with this donkey to save the inured soldiers. There was one who was blinded by a bandage, and Simpson helped him cross a muddy river. A bronze statue was made of this moment, and it is presented to the winners of the rugby league.

Reading Groups, stump your friends
with this one:
What was the donkey's name? (P.S. We
don't know the answer either, so make it up!)

27. The Somme of Us: How We Saved the Dirty French and They Never Even Thanked Us

AFTER THE WAR to End All Warts was over, our heroic boys also went off to defend the dirty French against the German Cyber Wilhelm, who was invasive.

We saved the French, our boys being the best soldiers in the world, but what did the French ever do for us in return?

Nothing but come and drop nuclear bombs in our backyard and grizzle that they had been the ones really who discovered us. If the French had discovered us, Australian men would kiss each other despite their garlic breath, Australian women would be oversexed and topless, and all people would be proud, arrogant etc. We would not speak English, which would be a great handicap with the Asians, New Zealanders, Fijians and Swedish backpackers.

Some historians say we shouldn't have saved

the French, but war is bunk and history is condemned to repeat itself etc (see chapter on World War Two later).

Moral for Focus Groups:
When you next think of whingeing,
think about it!

28. Billy-Bob Hughes: A Little Aussie Ditch Digger

BILLY-BOB HUGHES was our Pryminister during the War to End All Warts. He represented the Labor Party then he campaigned for Universal Circumcision and lost and he represented the Tory Party and campaigned for Universal Circumcision again and lost again then he was in the wilderness but he came back and was Pryminister for a third time though it was never certain for which party. Finally he went back into Labour.

Billy-Bob Hughes was our greatest wartime leader although some historians say he was a rat. Pictures show him wearing a range of distinguished hats.

From the Desk of Mr Slack:
Extra lunchtime tutorials available for 'cool' young Australians who 'dig' Aussie 'diggers'.

Quiz: Australia's Proud Military History

1. Who won the Bore Wore?

2. Who came second?

3. Snowy Breaker was a great:
   a. Horse handler.
   b. Ship's chandler.
   c. Faith bandler.
   d. Baby dandler.
   e. None of the above.

4. Who was the best Australian soldier?
   a. Sir John Potash.
   b. Wary Dunlop.
   c. Churchill.
   d. Simpson's Donkey.
   e. The one who was only 19.

5. When did Sydney sink?

6. In the Battle of Coral Tree, discuss the White Australia Policy.

7. Why don't the French sing Australia's national anthem every day?

8. Which do you prefer — Anzac Biscuits or Easter eggs? [Be careful.]

meet ur 4bears
(or: What if some great Aussies sent text messages from Beyond the Grave?)

King Charlesford Smith: 'Smithy'

hi there im Smithy & im an aviator
i flew airplanes in ww1 as a pilot in planes
made out of pianos & wire
i had 3 toes shot off by Germans who were
v v good shots
when there was no1 2 fight anymore, i 8 2
much then flew my Tiger Moth the Sthn X
roun tha world Bcoming the 1st person 2 x
the pacific unaided ie nonstop
i landed in Brizbn
unsatisfied i spent tha rest of my dayz flying
unaided nonstop
my chn wuz kidnapped & ransomed off while
i wuz away
i flew to Eng & back again, except 4 tha latter
. . . i perished in Bay of Bangle unaided . . .
ps i flew hi but never so hi as this place
where im now!!!!

29. Normal Lindsay: The Man who Loved Women and Children

NORMAL LINDSAY WAS a man who lived in the Blue Mountains and made Blue Movies. Most of them starred nude ladies, whom he loved, such as Elle Macpherson. He portrayed them in portraits with no clothes on and also *The Magic Pudding*.

The Magic Pudding showed that Normal Lindsay not only loved women but also children: the pudding, Albert, runs around with local identities Bunyip Bluegum, Sam Sawnoff and Barnacle Bill to escape from the pudding thieves who are codenamed Possum and Wombat. Albert gets a slice cut out of him but as soon as he does he grows it again! That's why he is magical. Like all those ladies, Albert became a model too, but he was an economic model.

Albert also had no clothes on, but he was a pudding.

'Talking Points' for Reading Groups:
What would it be like if no-one had any clothes on? Or just no pants?

30. Panic Depression

People still ask, 'What were the causes of Depression?' This is unknown as such, though the main cause was the Roaring Twenties and the Jazz Age. During their Roaring Twenties, people are generally very happy. They are young and dance a lot and for the first time in their lives they have some wealth to spend on gadgets.

The greatest poet of the Roaring Twenties is F. Scott Hemingway, who exceeded in excess of all else, thus typifying the spirit of the time. There was the Pro-Inhibition movement too, which said when people get drunk they are uninhibited, which is an embarrassment to all and sundries, so the best solution is to take their drinks away, at least before closing time.

So the six o'clock swell died out, and there was nothing left to drink. Many were in favour of Pro-Inhibition, but others were not, so they got sly grogged from speak easies and solar stills. It was a wild time because the world was awash with gadgets, jazz and hard liquor. Many gangsters made merry hell.

It all had to come to an end, and that end was Bloody Sunday which came after Black Tuesday and Ash Wednesday. Stock prices fell in a heap, ie you could get nothing for a good heifer nor a prize merino. We were trading too much with foreigners due to our end to protection rackets, and not even the Bank of England could save us, no matter how safe it appeared to be.

So all was bedlam. There was a Great Panic, and finally everyone was Depressed. No-one had a job and they all had to stand in line for their soup.

Millions of Australians lived in sea shanties on the edge of town, and they walked across the whole country for a crust of bread or a day's work. It is Depressing just to think about it. But it put lots of people into good habits, such as washing their gladwrap to re-use it, running their showers on cold water, weeing in the bush to save a penny, and in general the country was penny wise and pound foolish for the rest of their lives. Many years afterwards, old-timers would say Depression was the best thing that happened to them and the young could do with more Depression to teach them a lesson.

Moral for Focus Groups:
Life is meant to be easy . . . Not!

31. Our Don Bradperson: Now I Ask You Is He Any Good?

T HE ANSWER IS Yes! In fact, to set the record straight, he was VERY good!

People used to be able to call him Our Don Bradman, but in recent times Political Erectness set in, and he must be called Bradperson or, simply, Brad. Then on top of that he was Benighted, so he couldn't be Our Don anymore but we had to call him Sir Donald.

But that was all ahead of him when, as a boy born of poor but honest parents in the humble country town of Bowel, Young Don discovered his love of cricket. He homed his skills by hitting a golf ball with a toilet tank, though sometimes it hit him.

When he was young, Our Don hit his cricket critics for six! He played in Bowel at the Bradperson Oval which was his favourite oval, and he hit six sixes over the fence in an over. He faced the wiliest bowler in the land, Tiger Balm O'Reilly, and he hit him for six!

Don was picked for his state, and he scored 452 runs not out! And hit them all for six! And he bowled a few maidens over, I tell you!

Bowling Instructions for Focus Groups:
Line and length, line and length!

Young Don Bradperson homed his skills by hitting a golf ball with a toilet tank.

32. Bodyslime and the Rise of Hitler

WHEN THE COUNTRY had Depression, Young Don was their therapy. Like a strong relaxative pill he went through the Englishmen, hitting them all for six! And lightening the gloom!

But the Englishmen were a bad lot, and under their wicket captain Sardine, they came to Australia and tried to kill Bradperson with Bodyslime. (It was the same for our other great anti-Depressants, Far Lap and Less Darcy, whom everyone tried to kill all the time because they were too damn good.)

Sardine made his bowlers aim at Bradperson's head and his heart. But they were not very good shots, because they got poor old Bertie Oldfellow in the head and poor old Bill Gutfull in the heart. They missed Bradperson, and he hit them all for six!

What was going on out there? It was not cricket, that's what it was.

Yabbie was a man on the Hill, and he told it the way it was. When Sardine tried to brush a fly off his fly, Yabbie said: 'You leave our flies alone!' Though it was unclear which flies he meant.

Bill Gutfull said there are two crickets playing teams, but only one of them is not cricket. And that settled that. Bodyslime was banned and Sardine was sent home.

In Germany, Hitler did his own Bodyslime and became canceller.

Moral for Focus Groups:
That sucks.

33. World War 11

BECAUSE THE GERMANS were hell-bent on revision, it was inevitoral that there would be another War of the Worlds. The problem was that when the Germans attached other countries, everyone wanted to aplease them, because they were all scared of the Nasty Party and Uncle Adolf, who was the Fury. So he got the PM, Michael Chamberlain, to call him Uncle Adolf and everyone was charmed and calmed.

This policy ended up with the Germans attaching Poles, and enough was enough! Australia was at war.

At first it went badly, in the Phone War, when France lost (again). Part of France became Pre-occupied, and the rest had to drink Vichy water. Then the Germans attached Africa and held the Battle of Brittany.

Their main pilot was Rudolf Hessian who crashed into Scotland and was put into goal for the rest of his life, and this was where it all started to go wrong for the Nasties. They tried to attach

Russia but it had two fronts and that was the end of that.

Australia was in the war from the start, though this time we couldn't save the French because they couldn't save themselves. We were under greater threat from the Japanese, who were marching down from Asia in a Yellow Peril. The Australian soldiers were all thrown into Changa and put to work on the Burma Rail Road to Mandalay.

But Tojo never made it to Darwin. (Darwin is the home of Darwinism, a theory that if you leave people on their own for long enough they will return to Nature.)

Just when it all seemed lost, the Americans came in and saved us at the Battles of Middleway, Guacamole, Coral Tree and Okanui. As Macarthur had promised, he will returf, and returf he did.

God Bless America. If it wasn't for them we'd be eating sushi and driving Toyotas and playing video games. In gratitude for this, we now do whatever the Americans tell us and lucky too.

'Talking Point' for Reading Groups:
He who is your enemy's enema can be your friend's enemy's friend.

If it wasn't for General Macarthur, we'd all be eating sushi and driving Toyotas and playing video games.

34. The Attack of the Killer Midget Subs

SYDNEY CAME UNDER attack in the middle of World War 11. Two killer midget subs came into Sydney Harbour and bombed the HMAS *Cuttable*, which sank. The killer subs were captured and brought to justice and their sailors were tortured and given hurry curry.

Conspiracy Theory for Reading Groups:
Why did they only send two, and why were they not a better colour?
Have you ever thought about that?
Have you?????

35. The Rates of Tobruk

THE AUSTRALIANS WERE the greatest soldiers in World War 11. We beat the Germans at the Battle of the Bugle, which was the greatest tank battle ever. We beat the Germans also at the El Alamein Fountain, which was in Egypt. There we bogged down the famous Dessert Rat, Rommel. Rommel was in a song:

> *Hitler, he only had one ball,*
> *Rommel had two but they were small.*
> *Himmler had something sim'lar,*
> *But poor old Goballs had no balls at all.*

Nowadays we don't know what that means and it's been lost to history.

Moral for Focus Groups:
Focus groups suck.

36. Nancy Wakey-Wake: The Little Sparrow

NANCY WAKEY-WAKE was our greatest war heroin. As a child she jumped off a roof because her brother dared her to. Her mother said: 'So, if your brother told you he was jumping off a cliff, you would too?' Nancy said: 'Yes!'

She became less stupid later but no less brave. She was a pilot who flew for the Gestapo and bombed Germany. One night her plane crashed into the French resistance. She dressed up as a girl and worked undercover to save pilots from the Germans and spirit them back to happiness via Skegness. Her husband was also a member of the French assistance but he was killed by the Germans for not telling them where the Little Sparrow was. And he didn't know! She was a very independent woman, Nancy Wakey-Wake. After the war she led the feminist movement and got the vote.

Tip for Focus Groups:
Concentrate on the questions and you'll be able to go home earlier!

37. Bradperson's Last Balls

WITHOUT PEOPLE TRYING to kill him, Don Bradperson went on in his merrie waye, hitting all the bowlers for six! He smashed the English, squashed the South Africans, humbled the West Indies, and played cowboy to the Indians. He was Australia's greatest hero even though some records say he was a selfish bastard.

In 1948 he was an old man of 40 but he was coaxed out of retirement to lead the Unthinkables to England. There they won every match and hit their crickets for six! But poor Don Bradperson, in his last game he only needed to hit a four to make his average 100, and he tried to hit it for six! He missed, and was bowled for a googly. He couldn't help it though – he had a tear in his eye, which makes cricket a lot harder!

In retirement, Sir Donald Bradperson became a stockbroker and an endorser of hair care products and became filthy rich. He was the leading cricket administrator and exploited the working class, ie the players. But who were they to complain? Did they ever average 99.9999 repeater in the game? I don't think so!

When he died, Sir Donald Bradperson didn't give any interviews. He was a shy and retiring man and so was his son, Sir Johnald Bradperson, who changed his name to something else because he could not escape the shadow of his oldfellow.

Sir Donald Bradperson died tragically of pneumonia in 2001. He averaged 92 years old and was the Oldest Australian Ever.

'Talking Point' for Reading Groups:
Sir Donald Bradperson: Was he Great or did he Grate?

38. Wary Dunlop

Edward 'Wary' Dunlop was the Greatest
Australian Ever. He was born a sturgeon.
He grew up as a Victorian but was a born
leader. Everyone who knew him liked him, hence
his nickname.

He broke out World War 11 and ran the army
hospitals in the North African, Grecian and
Cretin campaigns. Then there were more hospitals and wars in Asia where he worked until he
was captured by the Japanese. So 'Wary' Dunlop
became a Pow-Wow.

Dunlop and the other Pow-Wows were taken
to build the Burma Shave railway line and Road
to Mandalay. They ate cold rice and rat meat and
had to stay awake for years. One man died for
every sleeper. They had maggots in their disintry
and their feet rotted in their boots or, if not, their
boots rotted on their feet. There was a lot of
bloody rot going on.

'Wary' Dunlop was their leader and their sturgeon, and he operated on them with sharpened

toothbrushes and bent spoons. Sometimes he cut their whole arms and legs off on purpose so they wouldn't have to work.

When the war was over, 'Wary' continued with his sturgeon work, though now he had better equipment. He cured cancer and helped the blind to see and made the Japanese feel better through forgiving them.

In 1977 he was Australian of the Year but really he was Australian of the Century!

Moral for Focus Groups:
Quick, get back in your chair,
here he comes!

meet ur 4bears
(or: What if some great Aussies sent text messages from Beyond the Grave?)

Howard Flora & Drugz

hello children u kin call me Ho-Flo coz im the Greatest Ozzie Ever dont believe what u hear about otherz

i dreamt of making sick people feel better coz i grew up in Adelaide

i met Ian Fleming the inventor of James Bond & penciln which stopped people dying of infractions

i got the gear

penciln was a mould Fleming discovered in a petrol dish of bacteria ie he ate it & it made him feel better like trippin out & stuff

i then giv it 2 mice & humans & it made them all feel like $1mil bling-bling!

i had 2 collect moulds from somewhere & my supplier wuz a T lady called Mouldy Mary who brought in her childrens socks undies rotten fruit jelly moulds etc.

i got tha Noble Priz 4 my work & then died . . . wish id tkn more a them drugz!!!

39. The Loyal Frying Doctor Service

AUSTRALIANS ALL LIVED in the outback and the black stump, so you might wonder what they did when they were sick. The answer was, they called Errol Flynn, 'Doctor Blood', who found the Loyal Frying Doctor Service.

Flynn was a swashbuckling hero, and when outback people were sick he flew on his own to fix them. He also brought God and Church to these savages, though he was also a legendary ladies' man, hence the saying, 'In Like Flynn of the Inland'. He dressed up as Robin Hood, Don Juan etc and entertained people with his brave sword fights. His favourite sayings were 'Laughter is the best medicine' and 'Oh Errol, I would give everything, just to be like him'.

At the end of his Hollywood career, sadly In Like Flynn of the Inland died. But they put his head on the $50 note.

Moral for Focus Groups:
You get what you paid for.

Errol Flynn found the Loyal Frying Doctor Service.

DON'T TRY THIS AT HOME!
Great Australian Inventions:
An Alternative History #1

To THE VICTA GO THE SPOILS.

Since the 1952 invention of the Victa lawn-mower by Mervyn Victor Richardson, the following injuries have been recorded by Australian hospitals:

- Loss of fingers ranging from one to six. (The six occurred when Lesley Arthur Cosgrove, 60, of Malvern, Victoria, lost all five fingers on his right hand reaching into his Victa to dislodge a garden stake that had become caught in the blades. He then lost the thumb of his left hand reaching in to try to retrieve one of his right hand's fingers.)

- Loss of toes ranging from one to five. (The first recorded toe lost to a Victa lawnmower was in 1953, in the first month of the mower going on general sale. Edward Lansky, 30, of Chullora, NSW, lost his left big toe when his Victa rolled backwards onto it from the force of his pulling the rip cord to start the motor.)

- Loss of eyes. (The most commonly reported Victa-related loss of sight was from pieces of blue metal or gravel being spat out at the user by the flying blades.)
- Loss of face. (A Japanese-Australian man, Shintaro McDonald, lost most of the right side of his face when bending down to see what was causing his Victa to malfunction. The lawn-mower began functioning perfectly well at that moment.)
- Back injuries. (The most common Victa-related injuries are to the back, ranging from badly pulled muscles to slipped discs to fractures, incurred while pulling the rip cord. It is estimated that for every one such reported injury, another 30–50 occur.)

40. Our Dawnie Fraser

OUR DAWNIE FRASER is not to be confused with Our Don Bradperson, who played a different sport. But they were both Ours. Dawnie Fraser was a swimmer who had a mind of her own. She left school because she didn't like being told what to do, and for reasons best known to herself she trained with her legs tied together and dragging a big steel drum. She crashed a car and her mum died. She thumbed her nose at officialdom. She got into further trouble when she marched at the Tokyo Olympics under the Japanese flag, which she had stolen from the Emperor's Palace. Our Dawnie was a lovable rouge and a politician and a Living Treasurer, but she was never really ours, she was hers.

> Moral for Focus Groups:
> No you don't.

41. Snugglepie and Cuddlepot

SNAGGLEPUSS AND COPPERPLATE were the creation of May Gibbs, whose brothers Barry, Maurice, Robin and Andy became most of the Bee Gees. May Gibbs was a children's book illustrator and her lovable characters were hung, drawn and quartered at her house in Sydney, called Nut Coat. The most frightening thing about May Gibbs was her paranoid fear of banksia. She thought they were big bad men with fat lips and nasty eyes, and they were chasing her around in the dark. She was committed to a mental asylum and she died without making her peace with banksia men and Aboriginals.

From the Desk of Mr Slack:
Who's talking up the back?

42. Economical Australia

AUSTRALIA'S ECONOMY HAS always ridden on the sheep's back.

Mining is the backbone of the country.

But we'll all be rooned said Hanrahan.

It's hard to make a crust let alone a brass razoo and under the poverty line the battlers aren't within a bull's roar of the hoi polloi.

But then they wouldn't work in an iron lung.

Such is life. Life wasn't meant to be easy.

Many people made their money on the bottom of the harbour. This was illegal so they were off quicker than a bride's nightie, shot through like a Bondi tram and went on the wallaby.

Our politicians are mad as a meathook and a drover's dog could do it. May their chooks turn into emus and kick their dunny down. They don't know if they're Artha or Marthur.

But she'll be right, mate, no worries.

Except things are crook in Tallarook.

Moral for Focus Groups:
Can we have lunch now?

43. The Age of Menzies' Eyebrows: Old

MENZIES WAS PRYMINISTER for so long they named a whole Error after him. It was called the Menzies Error.

Like most politicians, Menzies had very many opinions by the age of 12 and enjoyed talking down to people. He grew very fast which helped him in this regard. He studied hard and excelled at school and became a lawyer, then a politician, then Pryminister by the beginning of World War 2th.

When the Japanese threatened, he said, 'We will fight them on the beaches,' and many other inspirational speechifyings. He said 'Never before in the field of human combat'. Then he was sacked.

Menzies invented a new party which was called the Literal Party. It was on behalf of the people he called 'the forgotten people', who had been forgotten.

Soon he forgot them too. He figured out they could be easily scared. He ruled with a Pig-Iron

Fist and created scares in many colours such as the Red Scare and the Yellow Peril and Black Water Fever. He painted with a full palate of scary colours, that's for sure.

Menzies stayed in power all through the Menzies Error and even beyond. In 1966 he decriminalised the pound. In the 1960s he fell in love with the Queen when he did see her butt passing by. This was the love that dared not speak its name. When his love went unrequired, Menzies decided to go into the army and fight in Vietnam. He did not make it to Ho Chow Mein City himself but many others went there for him. They died and Menzies realised he had to retire or else the people would retire him.

The Menzies Error had long gone. And it was yet to come again.

'Talking Point' for Reading Groups:
What would you do with those eyebrows?
(Use a Mr Potato Head for illustration
if necessary.)

MESSER

Menzies fell in love with the Queen when he did see her
butt passing by.

44. The Petrol Affair

Mrs AND Mr Vladimir Petrol were spies who tried to get into Australia on a Norwegian ship called the *Tampon*. The Pryminister said they were terrists and wanted to come here to bomb us and cause events as shocking as 7–11. We were very frightened of them making a Petrol bomb or Molotov cocktail of drugs.

That year Christmas was a Thursday and the Petrols were sent to Nehru where they went on a hunger stroke. This was the Red Scare and White Australia didn't like it at all. When it turned into a big blue, Pig-Eye Bob got Black Jack onto it but he was too green.

Meanwhile on Nehru the Petrols sewed their eyelids together in protest. In the end the pacific solution to the problem was to put them into an asylum.

The Govment won the election.

'Talking Point' for Reading Groups:
What would you do if someone put Petrols around your house?

meet ur 4bears
(or: What if some great Aussies sent text messages from Beyond the Grave?)

jo'k aka tha wild 1

hey dudez im tha wild 1!!!!!

mbrando made this film bout me & me motrccl

i wuz a gr8 rock Rtist & me rock Rt wuz sold all tha way roun tha world

i wuz singer 4 the Btles + Lvis Prezly + mudD rivers +Tha Rollin St1s etc & cre8ed many gr8 big hits of rock Rt

i wore white leather chapsticks & crashed 1 car & wuz called v 'satur9'

soon tha pressure o fame Bcame 2 much tha Wild 1 retreated in2 his huge mansion & fell prey 2 a vicious cocktail o drugs + cocktails he blew up to twice his former size & referd 2 hmself in 3rd person & his bum looked big in everyfink

he defecated from tha Viet War & went 2 goal 4 Bing a conscious objector

he died o drink n drugs at a relatively tender age but sightings o him av Bn common ever since.

Part 4

the modem ERA

In the late 20th century Australia became a global nation, more rounded than ever before. We were happy and insulated in the Fifties, wild and rebellious in the Sixties, tasteless and selfish in the Seventies, flamboyant and crooked in the Eighties, and clichéd in the Nineties. Thus we were more and more like everyone else in the world, which was a bloody relief.

45. The Career War Path

A LITTLE-KNOWN WAR (which we also won) was the Career War. North Career and South Career were on the Career War Path for many years, even though they were proxy votes for the Russians, Chineses, Americans etc. This was part of the Cold War, which was so cold because it was fought in icy conditions in the north. In the Cold War places like Career became important.

Nothing much happened as both sides crissed and crossed over the Manson Dixon Line or the 38th Apparel as it was known to atlases. Nobody died, as it was a Cold War, and when it was over nothing changed.

But we won.

'Talking Point' for Reading Groups:
Was this the most boring war or what?

46. The Sydney Plush

HERE WE COME to a subject that should not be discussed in front of children.

The Sydney Plush was a secret society of wedgies and bodgies who shared radical ideas and bodily fluids.

They were very into stuffed toys, velvet cushions and other unspeakable items.

Many of the Plushies turned into conservatives.

They say that a conservative is a radical who has been mugged. But worse, much worse, had happened to those Plushies.

Moral for Focus Groups:
Sickening.

47. Vietnam: A Gorilla War

AUSTRALIANS WENT TO fight in Vietnam for eight reasons:

1. Vietnam was the Yellow Feral.
2. Vietnam was the Domino Theory.
3. Vietnam was the Commonest Block.
4. Vietnam was the one where the Duke killed them all in *The Green Berets*.
5. Vietnam had delicious food.
6. Vietnamese were all Boat People so they would be easybeats.
7. The Viet Cong was an invisible enemy.
8. The Americans told us to.

Pig-Eye Bob Menzies said okay, and Harold Holt who became Pryminister said ALL THE WAY FOR A BJ which was a pretty disgusting thing for an Australian Pryminister to say, but then that was our relationship vis a vis the American gun.

So thousands of young Australian boys went to

Vietnam seeking fame, fortune and a possible movie role in *The Dear Hunter*, *Full Mental Jacket*, *Pontoon* etc.

There was a bad disease communicable in Vietnam too, and this was made into a movie called *A Pox on me Lips Now*.

The worst part of Vietnam was Secret Agent Orange, which was a fruit pesticide spray that blew all over the place by mistake after the Americans did their crapdusting. As someone said, 'I love the smell of date palms in the morning!' but it wasn't date palms, it was Secret Agent Orange, which caused the Vietnam soldiers to develop birth infirmities such as extra heads and arms and not enough fingers and Thamodilide-ide. It gave them bad acidophilus flashbacks, which are good in movies but not so much when you have Secret Agent Orange, DDT, IUD and LBJ in your system. As they say, a Bad Trip.

So the Vietnam War was lost, producing a lot of Vietnam Vets which was good for local animals who needed care.

These Vets had long beards and rode motorbikes and suffered nightmares.

This was the only war we lost, so we like to call it something other than a war. We call it a conflict. So in wars we are still 6–0 but in conflicts 0–1.

Moral for Focus Groups:
War is Helicopters.

The Vietnam War was lost, producing a lot of
Vietnam Vets.

48. The Protest Movement

THE PROTEST MOVEMENT went up and down the main streets of Australia's cities. Protesters were consciousness objectors against the Vietnam War. They also didn't like the British doing their big nucular bomb experiments at Marijuana, in the South Australian dessert.

Their favourite symbol was the Peace Symbol and raising two fingers one way or the other. They burned their bras in protest against Vietnam. They grew long hair and looked like Jesus. They gave out love for free on Love-Ins. Their big heroes were Jack Lemmon of the Beatles and Germane Queer. They cared for the environment, saved the whales, obtained gray rights and other homosexual reformations, and unlike the Vietnam Vets they had good acidophilus trips (because they ate orgasmic foods and free rein chickens).

The main thing about the Protest Movement was that they were hippies. They all had idealistic ideals and they changed the world in order to make it easier for them to then go and get a job and buy a house and get rich on the stockmarket and Run the Show. Which they did. After they finished the Protest Movement, they went home and were Booby Beamers.

'Talking Point' for Reading Groups:
Those people suck so bad.

DON'T TRY THIS AT HOME! Great Australian Inventions: An Alternative History #2

THE HILLS HEIST.

On 30 March 1971, John Curry, 21, of Perth, and Brett Scott, 17, also of Perth, were arrested and charged with trespass, attempted robbery and damage to property following an incident in the suburb of East Perth.

Curry and Scott had been engaged in what one neighbour described as a 'long-running feud' with a neighbour, Mr Colin Suggs, 44. Mr Suggs lived in a one-bedroom fibro house between the residences of Curry and Scott.

On the night of 29 March 1971, police allege Curry and Scott trespassed onto Suggs's property, climbing a wooden fence to his backyard. While Suggs slept in the house, Curry and Scott cut through the base of Suggs's Hills Hoist, shearing it from the ground. Police told Perth Local Court that they proceeded to pack the 'hollow stem' of the clothes line with approximately five pounds of TNT explosives and gunpowder.

They then rested the Hills Hoist at a 45 degree angle against a wooden sawhorse they had procured from Mr Suggs's back shed, police told the court, and pointed the 'nose' of the clothes line at the house. They fixed a fuse to the explosives and lit it, allegedly with the intention of propelling it in the direction of the sleeping Mr Suggs's bedroom.

The Hills Hoist flew a short distance, its stays making contact with the rear of the dwelling, without breaching its asbestos skin. Curry and Scott subsequently fled the scene but were later apprehended by police responding to a call from the alarmed Mr Suggs.

A police spokesman said: 'The only reason the Hills Hoist failed to fly was that they didn't put enough dynamite in there. It needed twice the amount. Mr Suggs was only a few ounces of forward thinking between here and Kingdom Come.'

Curry and Scott were remanded on bail of $5,000.

49. Harold Holt and the Shark Alarm Murders

Harold Holt was the Pryminister after Pig-Eye Bob. Harold Holt was a good friend of the Americans and took us further into Vietnam. This made him a terrist target in case the Vietnamese invaded us, so to be safe Harold Holt used to wear a frog suit and hide in the waters off the Melbourne beach of Curtsea.

One afternoon he was diving in his frog suit and he never came back. He did what was termed a 'Harold Holt'. His wife, Dam Zara Bait, was put into the water as chum but no result.

'Talking Point' for Reading Groups:
Who took Harold Holt? Debate whether it
was a UFO, the CIA, the VC, Jaws,
Neptune or Davey Jones's Locker.
Supplementary question: Where did
he/it/they put him?

Quick Quiz:
The Australian Film Industry

1. A great Aussie film was 'Dad and ...':
   a. Dadder.
   b. Mum.
   c. Carol and Ted and Alice.
   d. Dave.

2. Who has starred as Ned Kelly?
   a. Mick Jagger.
   b. Keith Richards.
   c. Peter Carey.
   d. Leaf Hedger.
   e. Himself.

3. When was the great Aussie Fillum Revival?
   a. 1780s.
   b. 1920s.
   c. 1960s.
   d. TBA.

4. Annette Kellerman was:
   a. A model.
   b. A model-cum-singer.

   c. A model-cum-singer-cum-swimmer.

   d. A model-cum-singer-cum-swimmer-
       cum-actress.

   e. More of the above.

5. Phil Noyce's first great film was:

   a. Newsfront.

   b. Newspeak.

   c. Broadcast News.

   d. Behind the News.

   e. Network.

6. Match the director with the Aussie film:

   1. Peter Weird.

   2. Fred Septic.

   3. Bruce Hereford.

   4. Gilligan Armstrong.

   5. Henry Miller.

   a. Droving Miss Daisy.

   b. Little Ladies.

   c. Picnic at How's It Hanging Rock.

   d. Mad Macca.

   e. Very Very Very Very [No Exceptions] Last
      Orders.

7. 'Priscilla Queen of the Dessert' was:
   a. A Queen.
   b. A Drag Queen.
   c. A Dessert.
   d. A Bus.
   e. A Bust.

8. In 'Strictly Ballroom', who gets the girl?
   a. The guy.
   b. The dad.
   c. The friend.
   d. The other girl.
   e. The dance.
   f. No it doesn't end that way.

9. Narrow the eyes to a squint and spot the
   Australian:
   a. Russell Crowe.
   b. Nicole Kidman.
   c. Greg Norman.
   d. Peter Finch.
   e. Jane Campion.

10. Complete this sentence: 'Australian films ...':
    a. Suck.
    b. Are the best in the world bar none.
    c. Suck the best in the world bar none.
    d. Offer value for money.
    e. Such as The Matrix and Star Wars are great, but the rest suck.
    f. Are undoubtedly of high artistic merit and entertainment value but I cannot speak with authority as it's been a long while since I've seen one.

50. John Gorton, Still Jolly After Being Done in the Back by Bug-Eyes McMahon and That Dog Fraser

SIR JOHN GORTON was Australia's greatest Pryminister. He was a fighter pilot in World War 11 when he flew Mosquitoes and nailed Fritz and Tojo. He liked a drink and had a pug's nose. He had an affair with Adele Weiss which made him more colourful.

Unfortunately men of such greatness and heroism cannot last long in Canberra, where people prefer them to be slimy and dishonest. So Sir John Gorton was knifed in the back by Billy McMahon and Malcolm Fraser, who turned out to be the worst and the second worst Pryministers we ever got. Sir Jolly John retained his sense of humour, however, and went on to become our greatest ex-Pryminister ever.

Moral for Focus Groups:
We'll sort him out for you, John.

Don't Try This At Home!
Great Australian Inventions:
An Alternative History #3

THERE HAS BEEN one occasion when seven unique Australian inventions have been combined in the one, disastrous experiment. The inventions were: The Wine Cask, The Wiltshire Staysharp Knife, The Bionic Ear Implant, The Winged Keel, The Pop-Top Can, In-Vitro Fertilisation, and Permanent Press Trousers. For legal reasons, we are not permitted to disclose the exact nature or consequences of this experiment.

Quick Quiz:
Great Australian Inventions

Which of these Australian inventions should
NEVER be mixed up in the same sentence?

a. The Orbital Engine and the Heart Pacemaker.
b. Speedo Swimwear and the Super Sopper.
c. The Wiltshire Staysharp Knife and the Inflatable
   Aircraft Escape Slide.
d. Sportswool and the Footrot Vaccine.
e. The Reading Machine for the Blind and
   Race Cam.

51. Cough Whitlam: It's Time

Aꜰᴛᴇʀ Hᴀʀᴏʟᴅ Hᴏʟᴛ was eaten by a UFO, there was a succession of Bad Pryministers such as Bug-Eyes McMahon.

In 1972 the people were in the mood for a change, and they sang a song called 'It's Time'. The words were:

> *It's Time for Something/*
> *It's Time for Something/*
> *It's Time/*
> *for Something/*
> *It's TIME!*

It was composed and sung by Cullough McColleen and everybody was in on it including Bob Hawk who was drunk.

The smell had become so strong that the people elected Van Gogh Whitlam, the first labourer Pryminister in 23 long years.

Van Gogh Whitlam was a very arrogant and brainy man who was also tall, so it was a miracle anyone elected him. He set up a junta of two with Vance Packard and together they changed all the laws in 100 days. This was known in leafy suburbs as The Great Terror.

Van Gogh Whitlam made universities free, and paid artists and singers the highest social wages in the land, and a hippie, Jim Cairns, was the treasurer so all the money went to mung bean farmers, tie-dye artists and anti-war protesters who burnt bras.

It was time all right! High times!

Everyone had free love, including Cairns who was doing it with his secretary Junie Morose, and Bob Hawk who was doing it with everyone else.

Cough Whitlam went to China and he recognised it.

Cough Whitlam went to Indonesia and was craven when they killed Australian journalists.

But Cough's biggest mistake was the Home Loans Affair. His mining minister was a man named Jimmy Connors who got involved with a shady businessman called Ken Leilani. Connors borrowed Home Loans from Leilani that came from the Middle East in petrodollars. This money had been sold as arms-for-oil deals between the

CIA and the Americans and the Iran Contras. The story is too complicated to go into now, but when the Opposition found out about Ken Leilani they blocked Supply, which meant the govment had no money, which meant they had to go back to Leilani and ask for more to pay off the Governor-General.

But the Governor-General at that time was a great Lion with a white main of hair called Sir John Cur, and he wore a top hat over his white main and a coat with tails. He rose above the struggle and decided to sack Cough Whitlam behind his back.

When Cough found out he uttered his immortal speech: 'God may save well, but the Queen will save the Governor-General'.

Nobody knew what Cough was going on about, so when they got an election with a Double Disillusion, they booted him out.

'Talking Point' for Reading Groups:
Does Cough Whitlam do birthday parties?

GUESS WHO?
Great Australians Come Play 20 Questions!

1788: Your full name please?

X: You won't get me that easily.

1788: Your special subject?

X: Mon sujet, c'est moi.

1788: Are you French?

X: No but the world does revolve around me.

1788: Are you animal, vegetable or mineral?

X: It's debatable, but more animal or mineral than vegetable.

1788: What is your greatest contribution to the nation?

X: I was going to say all the taxes I'd paid, but then . . . Hahahahaha!

1788: Are you a businessman?

X: That's what they say.

1788: What do you say?

X: Was that another question?

1788: Was what?

X: Was that too?

1788: What?

X: ?

1788: Okay ... What do you most love about our great nation?

X: Its politicians.

1788: And our democratic institutions?

X: Depends.

1788: On what?

X: On my say-so.

1788: Where do you live?

X: None of your business.

1788: Gotcha.

X: Got what?

1788: I'm asking the questions here, Mr Murdoch.

Quiz: The 20th Century

1. Using either [a] the Shark Arm Murders, [b] the Beaurepaire children, [c] Azaria Chamberlain, or [d] the Dingo, solve the mystery of Harold Holt's disappearance. Use no more than three lined pages.

2. Phar Lap was:
   a. Hoarse.
   b. Less Darcy.
   c. Dead.
   d. Large of Heart and Spleen.
   e. Girt by Sea.

3. In his last inning, Bradperson scored:
   a. Zero.
   b. Zip.
   c. Duck.
   d. Blob.
   e. Egg.
   f. 99.94.

4. If Captain Bligh, Ned Kelly, Billy Hughes, Donald Bradperson, Wary Dunlop, Nancy Wakey-Wake, Cullough McColleen and Phar Lap were in a cage fight, who would win and why?

5. Patrick Write word association:
   a. Nobleman.
   b. Noble Prize.
   c. Noble intentions.
   d. Nobbled.
   e. Nobbed.
   f. Nob.

6. When did the 1960s arrive in Australia?
   a. The 1960s.
   b. The 1970s.
   c. The 1980s.
   d. The 1990s.
   e. The 2000s.
   f. Not yet.

7. 'Red Ted, Black Jack and White Australia'. Please explain.

8. Should Australians:
    a. Buy Australian?
    b. Buy South Australian?
    c. Buy The Australian?
    d. Bye-bye Australia?

9. Which was the best Holden?
    a. FJ.
    b. BJ.
    c. FH.
    d. B&H.
    e. E-Type.
    f. G.
    H. i.

10. Name one person on one Australian money bill [triple points].

11. What, who or why were BS St Aloysius and the Catholic Spliff?

12. Name a member of the Sydney Plush [double points for naming none].

13. Who was most Australian?
    a. Slim Dusty.
    b. Smokey Dawson.
    c. Chad Morgan.
    d. Lee Kernaghan.

14. Spot the Australian actor [triple points]:
    a. Nicole Crowe.
    b. Russell Kidman.
    c. Peter Flynch.
    d. Errol Finn.
    e. None of the above.
    f. All of the above.
    g. Don't know.
    h. Do know but won't say.
    i. Don't care.
    j. Undecided.
    k. Combination of the above [explain].
    l. Other [explain].

52. The Mambo Treaty

Eddie Mambo was a black fellow born in the Torrid Straight. He and his best friend Murray Ireland had been hunting and fishing for a long time before the White Man came to claim his land writes. Eddie Mambo and Murray Ireland became active in activism, and soon they got the vote.

Mambo realised one day that he and other peoples from the Horrid Traits actually owned their islands even though they were Crown Lamb. This was the origin of Terror Nullarbor. As if that wasn't confusing enough, other people from the Sorry States Islands had been fishing there for generations and had possession, occupation, use and enjoyment, which was all they needed and all anyone could hope for in this day and age.

So it all went to the highest court in the land, namely the Hire Court. Eddie Mambo's greatest moment came at the end of that case when the Hire Court said 'yes, Eddie, you are the owner of the Mambo Islands'. Unfortunately Eddie died of cancer six months earlier.

> Moral for Focus Groups:
> And so we come full circle . . .
> (discuss)

GUESS WHO?
Great Australians Come Play 20 Questions!

1788: Are you male or female?
X: Female.
1788: In what century were you born?
X: 20th.
1788: Are you alive or dead?
X: For me to know and for you to find out.
1788: How famous are you?
X: Fame is fickle.
1788: Do you like jewellery?
X: I love things that glitter.
1788: What is your IQ?
X: Off the scale.
1788: Do you have a pet?
X: Never liked animals.
1788: Are you Joan Sutherland?
X: Bzzz.
1788: Do you sing?
X: No but I squeal like blue murder.

1788: What's your favourite colour?

X: Black.

1788: What's your favourite leisure activity?

X: Camping.

1788: What's your favourite clothing?

X: Terry towelling.

1788: Do you believe in God?

X: I used to.

1788: Are you Azaria Chamberlain?

X: About time you found me.

53. Pauline Howard: the Dear Leader

Pauline Howard was Australia's Pryminister in the 1990s. She was known for her eye-catching opinions and outspoken hair. She was a very ordinary Australian, and spoke up for others of her ilk.

Pauline Howard was always interesting. She was the Federal Trash'n'Treasurer in the 1970s when she achieved record high interest ratings. She served her time in the wilderness in the 1980s, just like in the Bible, and as Opposition Leader she banned Asian immigration, migration, emigration, transmigration etc. In fact she said 'Enough is Enough!' and banned all Asian foodstuffs, galangal, lemongrass, Hoisin sauce, and other pollutants such as derivative pop tunes.

Pauline owned a fish shop so she was a healthy eater and spoke for the virtues of white meat. She was pure as the drivel snow and firmly in the mainstream of mainstream Australia. She didn't like people getting handouts for nothing and told the Aboriginals and Asians to 'Go back where you came from!'

Pauline was famous for her catchy sayings, such as 'Please Explain?'. But nobody explained anything to her, so you can't be blame her for asking.

When she became Pryminister, Pauline Howard saved Australia for the Australians and kept out the riff raff. She had a rap song named after her and did dancing on TV. She was beloved of the male members of the house and gave them premature elections.

**Moral for Focus Groups:
None here.**

54. The Rest

Whitlam maintained the rain against Fraser, but he lost and became the name of a popular band, The Goughs.

The Seventies happened, and then the Eighties, which were the decade that taste forgot and the Me decade respectively. The Eighties was a time of shoulderpads and entrecotes such as Bond, Skaife, Homes O'Court, and other West Australians who were all criminals. Then came the crash of '87 which was known as Black Monday, or Black Tuesday.

Australia was the flavour of the month and Paul Hogan threw a shrimp on the barbie for us all and the Japanese came and bought the farm then sold it again.

In the Nineties we became a global Asian nation under Bob Hawk and Paul Heating, and then we became a British one again under Pauline Howard.

We nearly had a People's Republic of Austria but it was defeated in a referendum because too many people wanted it. We had reconciliation but then, not.

We had Mambo and Wick but then, not.

We had the tragedy of 7–11 and so we declared War on Error, which was a good thing because we'd always been afraid of Error, ever since Terror Nullius and the fear of Jimmy Blacksmith and Ned Kelly and Red Ted Theodore and the Black Flash and the Yellow Peril and White Australia and the Rainbow Worrier and the Franklin Dam and the Stormin' and Packer and *On the Waterfront* and the Unions and the Commies and the Domino Theory and Charlie and Inflation and Drugs and Bali and Dole Bludgers and Pilates and the Glasshouse Effect and everyone else we'd always been afraid of, they were all Error, so it was a very good thing indeed that we would set out to stomp it all out in a Great Big War to End All Warts.

Moral for Focus Groups:
It happened.

55. Conclusion: The End of Australian History

MOST HISTORIANS BELIEVE the end of Australian history is not in sight although some believe it has already come and gone and others still say Australian history has not yet begun, or there is not enough of it, so how can it be ending, or even be in sight of the beginning of the ending, or some would say the end of the beginning?

As always in history, there is room for mass debate.

What cannot be debated is that we are a Young Nation and a Lucky Country if Sunburnt and therefore at risk of skin canker. So all in all, the future looks bright as long as we look after the past, because the past is our present to the future.

All that remains to be said, in or preferably out of tune of 'Hey True Blue' played by a strumming acoustic guitar with the sun setting over the black stump and the waves crashing on the sandy shores and the sea girting our wealth for toil:

'I am, you are, we are Australian, and we are history.'

Reader Satisfaction Survey

1. How satisfied are you?
   a. Very satisfied.
   b. Quite satisfied.
   c. Satisfied.
   d. Not quite satisfied.
   e. Not very satisfied.

2. Rate Australian history out of ten.

3. What is your reaction to this: Bug-Eyes McMahon and Malcolm Fraser were bastards who knifed Sir John Gorton in the back and stole the Pryministership?
   a. Very strongly agree.
   b. Strongly agree.
   c. Agree strongly.
   d. Agree very strongly.

4. In fewer than six words, name your favourite character from Australian history and why.

5. Please offer three suggestions for how Australian history can be improved. Provide, where possible, a business plan.

6. Please conceptualise, design, produce and fund a nationwide all-media advertising and marketing campaign promoting Australian history in general and this book in particular. [Unlimited bonus points for getting this correct.]

7. How's it going? [Please answer by age, state and socioeconomic class.]
   a. Good.
   b. Very well, thank you.
   c. Fine thanks, and you?
   d. Orright.
   e. What's it to you?
   f. Bugger off.
   g. Don't know.

General reader consumer survey so we can contact you during dinner-time:

1. Do you shop for food?

2. Would you describe yourself as:
   a. 14-57
   b. 58 and above?

3. Do you drive?

4. Do you drive well?

5. Do your friends consider you attractive?

6. Do you consider your friends attractive?

7. Do you give money readily to people who call you during dinner-time, as a way of getting rid of them?

8. Which carrier takes your long-distance calls?

9. Have you ever invested in Nigeria?

10. Have you considered trying to hypnotise women?

11. Could you do with some extra inches?

12. What is your education level?

12a. Do you want a university diploma delivered within days?

13. Have you ever read a book?

14. Have you ever seen a grown man naked?

15. Have you committed any fatal terrorist attacks? Non-fatal?

16. Do you intend to carry small firearms on an international flight this year?

17. Do you think you know it all already?

18. Do you think surveys should continue until they reach a round number of questions?

19. What do you consider to be a round number?